Landscaping
New Homes

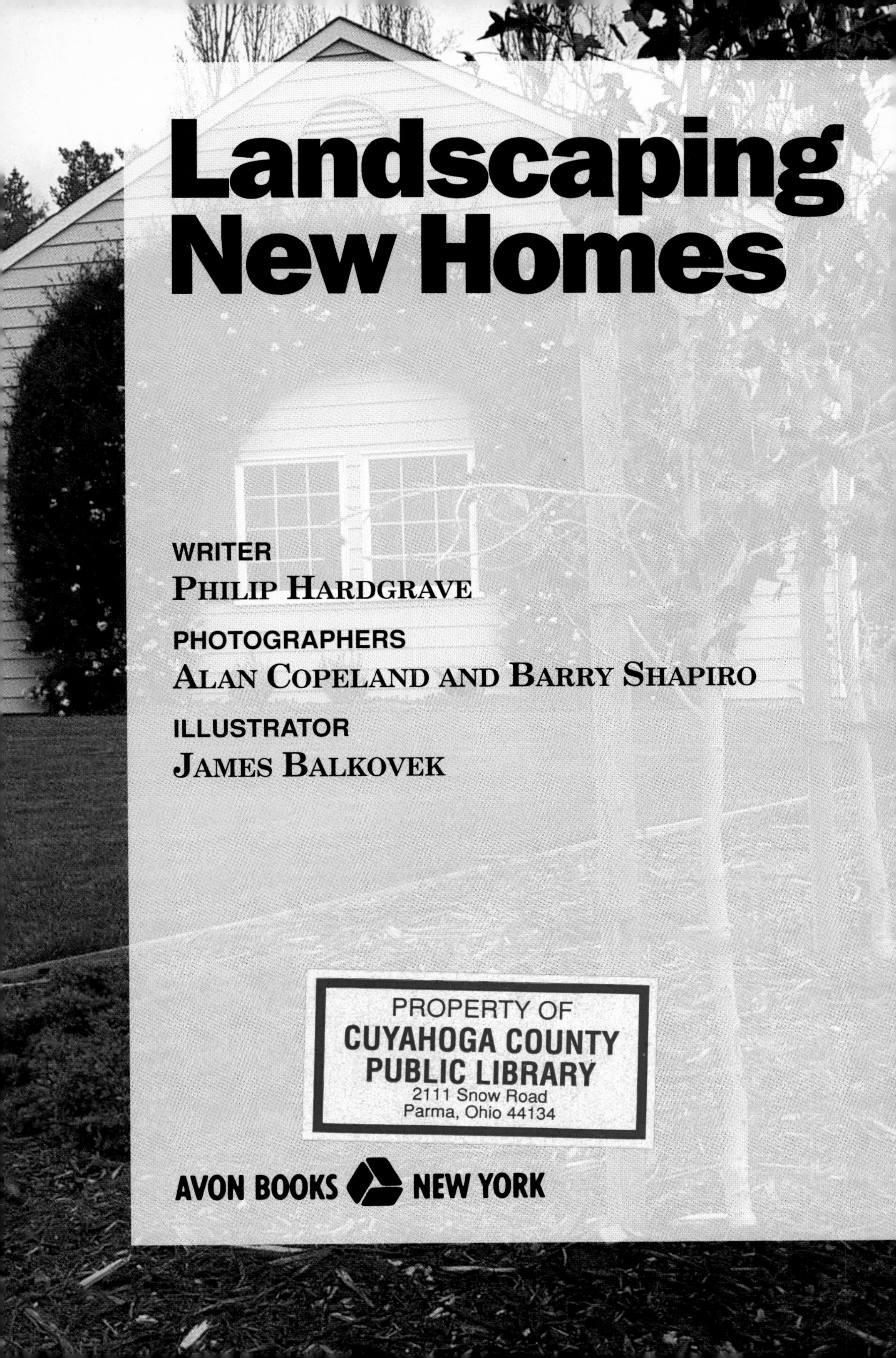

Landscaping New Homes

WRITER

Philip Hardgrave

PHOTOGRAPHERS

Alan Copeland and Barry Shapiro

ILLUSTRATOR

James Balkovek

AVON BOOKS ◆ NEW YORK

Product Manager: CYNTHIA FOLLAND, NK LAWN & GARDEN CO.

Acquisition, Development and Production Services: BMR, Corte Madera, CA

Acquisition: JACK JENNINGS, BOB DOLEZAL

Series Concept: BOB DOLEZAL

Project Director: JANE RYAN

Developmental Editor: JILL FOX

Horticulturist: BARBARA STREMPLE

Landscape Design and Horticultural Consultant: RG TURNER JR

Photographic Director: ALAN COPELAND

Art Director (cover): KARRYLL NASON

Art Director (interior): BRAD GREENE

Cover Design: KAREN EMERSON

Cover Styling: JOANN MASAOKA VAN ATTA

Cover Photo: BARRY SHAPIRO

Cover Landscape Design: PETER KOENIG DESIGNS OF DANVILLE

Interior Art: JAMES BALKOVEK

Landscape Plans: RG TURNER JR

Site Scouts: PEGGY HENRY, RG TURNER JR, PAT TALBERT

Photo Assistant: LISA PISCHEL

Copy Editor: JANET VOLKMAN

Proofreader: LYNN FERAR

Typography and Page Layout: BARBARA GELFAND

Indexer: SYLVIA COATES

Color Separations: PREPRESS ASSEMBLY INCORPORATED

Printing and Binding: PENDELL PRINTING INC.

Production Management: THOMAS E. DORSANEO, JANE RYAN

92 93 94 95 96 10 9 8 7 6 5 4 3 2 1

First Avon Books Trade Printing: February 1993

Library of Congress Cataloging-in-Publication Data:
Hardgrave, Philip.
    Landscaping new homes / writer, Phil Hardgrave; photographers, Alan Copeland and Barry Shapiro, illustrator James Balkovek.
        p. cm. – (NK Lawn & Garden step-by-step visual guide)
    Includes index.
    ISBN: 0-380-76803-8
    1. Landscape gardening. 2. Landscape architecture. I. Title. II. Series.
SB473.H358 1993
712'.6–dc20   92-18620
                                                        CIP

Special thanks to the following landscape designers for their assistance with sites: Patricia Posner, Kentfield, CA (pgs. 1; 9, low-maintenance garden; 11, bench; 42, picket fence); Stauffacher Solomon/Strang (pg. 12, play area); David A. Schwartz, Schwartz Associates, Sausalito, CA (pgs. 54–55); Cynthia Egger, Larkspur, CA (pgs. 34–35, 46–47). Also, Alden Lane Nursery, Livermore, CA (pgs. 60–61) and San Benito House, Half Moon Bay, CA (pg. 9, cottage garden).

Also special thanks to: Strybing Arboretum & Botanical Garden and Golden Gate Park, San Francisco, CA; Blake Estate, UC Berkeley, CA; McPhails Building Materials, Sonoma, CA; Napa County Resource Conservation District; Roger Raiche; Galen Fultz; Mary Chomenko and Greg Hinkley; Katherine Kirk; Janet Pischel; Maria Poindexter; Kathie Feidler; Rocky Marco; and Anne Wagner.

Additional photo credits: Saxon Holt, (pg. 12 dog run); Derek Fell (pg. 65, ivy).

Notice: The information contained in this book is true and complete to the best of our knowledge. All recommendations are made without any guarantees on the part of the authors, NK Lawn & Garden Co., or BMR. Because the means, materials and procedures followed by homeowners are beyond our control, the author and publisher disclaim all liability in connection with the use of this information.

AVON BOOKS
A division of
The Hearst Corporation
1350 Avenue of the Americas
New York, New York 10019

AVON TRADEMARK REG. U.S. PAT. OFF. AND IN OTHER COUNTRIES, MARCA REGISTRADA, HECHO EN U.S.A.

TABLE OF CONTENTS

MAKING EARLY DECISIONS

STEPS TO A LANDSCAPE

The interiors of new houses are usually ready for furniture when the owner arrives, but the yard is rarely ready for planting. To start off on the right foot, familiarize yourself with the basic steps of landscape planning and installation.

The purpose of landscaping a home is to provide a functional space that is pleasing to look at. Landscaping will solve site problems that may exist in the yard, expand the living area of your home, increase the property value and provide a space in which you and your guests can relax and enjoy life.

The landscape consists of the *hardscape* and the *greenscape*. Hardscape features are built fixtures such as utilities—lighting and irrigation—and structures—paths, decks, patios, walls and fences. The greenscape is the plants—trees, shrubs, groundcovers, grasses, vines and annual and perennial flowers. Both require thorough planning before construction and installation occur.

Although every project is unique, the basic steps are the same for every landscape. The contents of this book follow the steps to a landscape used by professional landscape designers and installers. Use the page headings to develop your project schedule. A well thought out schedule ensures that everything that needs doing actually gets done.

LANDSCAPE DESIGN

Landscape design is an art based on the same principles as other types of art. These principles are form, scale, rhythm, axis, color and texture. Form is the shape and structure of the elements. Too much of one form—all rectangles, for example—will be monotonous; too many different forms can become confusing. Vertical forms present a sense of awe; horizontal forms, peacefulness; straight lines, reason; intricate forms, curiosity; curves, harmony; circular forms, closure; jagged forms, power.

Scale refers to relative size. When choosing the size of various elements, consider the size of the house, lot and people using it.

Rhythm refers to ordering elements in the landscape, like beats in music. Give your landscape rhythm by repeating similar forms in the same scale or the same construction materials and plants in various areas.

Axis gives a landscape visual orientation, forcing people to look at what you want them to see. Axis is formed by paths, paving patterns, lighting and plants that hide, frame or create views.

Cool colors, such as green and blue, recede, making a yard look larger. Warm colors, such as red and orange, pop out, making the space seem smaller. Use the same color palette outdoors as in the house interior to unify the two areas. Consider how the colors will work together over the length of an entire year. Many deciduous plants turn from spring green to autumn red to winter brown. These seasonal changes should be incorporated into your landscape design.

Texture refers to the visual and tactile surfaces of all materials used in your design. Combine different textures in the hardscape and greenscape to add interest. Smaller spaces are more conducive to fine-textured elements; larger ones to coarser textures.

Hardscape construction and greenscape installation can be spread over a number of years as time and finances allow.

7

CHOOSING A LANDSCAPE THEME

Traditional American Symmetrical gardens arranged in a formal pattern around the house create a theme suitable for most house styles and regions. Gravel or brick paths enclose separate vegetable and flower garden areas, lined by sheared hedges and fronted by a white picket fence.

Moorish The courtyard garden usually features a fountain or pool as a centerpiece, with ceramic tile or patterned brick accenting the patio surface and high, enclosing garden walls providing privacy. Moorish landscape themes are well suited to dry climates and drought-resistant plantings.

Oriental Water, wood and stone are used to set off seemingly casual groupings of carefully shaped conifers and shrubs in an atmosphere of quiet and seclusion. This garden theme calls for asymmetrical planting patterns complemented by statuary, lanterns and bamboo fencing.

Cottage Informal flower beds, massed shrubbery and winding earthen or gravel paths invite the visitor into the rustic cottage setting, creating a relaxed but colorful environment with an earthy feeling. Cottage gardens work well with small yards and houses of wood, stone or stucco design.

Native Plants, native grasses and groundcovers adapted to the local climate are used to create a smooth, natural transition between the surrounding area, the garden and the domestic interior. Native gardens fit in with rustic housing styles of almost any region and climate.

Low-Maintenance A combination of paved paths and patios, indigenous plants and drip irrigation systems with timer controls, means less work for the homeowner. Plan all or part of the landscape as low-maintenance to lessen long-term gardening chores.

GETTING IDEAS

A successful landscape theme is a well-planned, coordinated combination of hardscape and greenscape based on a single design motif. Get your ideas from a variety of sources. Browse through gardening books, clip photographs from magazines and visit and photograph public gardens and the yards of friends and family. Walk through your neighborhood and see how others in your immediate area have landscaped their new houses.

Before settling on a theme, consider how it will accentuate the architectural style of the house. The theme should complement the interior and exterior style of the house, particularly where there is a direct transition from house to yard. If you have a definite interior design theme, consider expanding that theme to the landscape for a complete look.

Use the scale of the house to determine the scale of outside activity areas, and the interior color palette when choosing colors for the exterior. Consider building materials used in the house for use in the landscape. If the house has a brick siding, for example, use brick paving materials for paths, edgings or planter boxes to tie the house and yard together.

As you open your eyes to the world of landscape design themes, you will discover ones that you prefer and features that you would like to duplicate in your yard. Begin a file of design ideas—an accordion file works well—to organize the photographs and clippings you collect. Use these ideas for inspiration as you put together your landscape plan.

CHOOSING FEATURES

MAKING A WISH LIST

The purpose of a landscape design is to turn what you have into the yard of your dreams. A useful aid in the design process is a wish list. Write your wish list to include everything you ever wanted in a landscape.

Include needed site corrections and the level of maintenance you feel fits your life-style and desired social and gardening activities. Although you may not obtain every desired item in one yard, it costs nothing to list it. Have everyone who will use the yard contribute ideas to the wish list. In addition to contributing ideas, participants can suggest how ideas can be combined into other ideas.

There are no bad ideas at this point; use the wish list as a brainstorming tool. The wilder the idea the better; it is easier to tame down an idea later than to dream one up. Go for a quantity of ideas, because the more ideas you have the more likely you'll find useful ones. Later, space requirements and budget restrictions will narrow down the list to the essentials.

Take time to develop your wish list over several months, if possible. Imagine the yard throughout the year and how your needs for it will be different on a hot summer day as compared to a cold winter night.

Your list will be specific to your landscape and your life-style. You probably will not be able to fit everything in the final design. However, dreaming is free, and that is the point of the wish list.

Entertaining Available in many styles and sizes, gazebos can be bought in kits or custom designed and built. As an extra room in the garden, gazebos are useful for open-air dining and providing shelter from summer showers.

Attracting Animals Small pools or fountains for birds to drink from or bathe in are a popular landscape feature. Whether you purchase it or build it yourself, a birdbath should be designed as an attractive piece of outdoor sculpture.

Gardening Features Set a container of flowers in the windowsill or wall alcove as a picturesque display. Plants can be viewed from inside and out and should be easily reached for watering and pruning.

Relaxing A secluded bench, hammock or low wall is a perfect rest area for anyone trying to get away from it all. The garden retreat should be far enough from other activity that anyone reading, resting or contemplating the garden is undisturbed.

SPECIAL FEATURES

Your choices of landscape features should be based on practical and utilitarian requirements as well as suitability to the landscape theme. The right selection and installation of structures and amenities will expand the usable living space, provide access to different areas of the yard and enhance the beauty and charm of the property.

When establishing your wish list you may list specific features you want in your yard or simply activities you want to enjoy there. Either way, there is a host of features available to use in your yard; some are shown on these and the following pages.

If you want to use your landscape for entertaining, consider how you want to entertain, the most practical area in the yard for it and the amount of space you need to do it. Entertaining is usually done on a patio, deck, gazebo or lawn, perhaps near the kitchen or living room for combined indoor and outdoor parties. Entertaining areas should include a gas line for a barbecue, water lines for an outdoor bar, lighting for nighttime parties, seating and table room and flat areas for sports.

Attracting birds and other animals is a popular reason to landscape. Select locations for birdbaths and bird and animal feeders where the animals can be safe from predators and where you can view these visitors without disturbing them. Plant flowers that attract birds and beneficial insects into your yard. Conversely, you may need to design fencing and plantings to discourage animals from coming in. High fences and thorned shrubs help keep unwanted deer and dogs from entering.

MEETING NEEDS

Do not split your plan between pretty and practical. Landscape features that serve a practical purpose also can be visually interesting. Use the principles of design and your theme to coordinate these features in your landscape.

Play Area Activity areas for children should be visible from the house for adult supervision. Meet the needs of children of different ages with separate areas. Install soft treatments such as sand under play structures.

Pet Needs Exercise areas and pens for dogs and other animals need to be secure but accessible. High fences keep your pet in and other animals out of your new landscape.

Vegetable Gardening Herb and vegetable gardens may need to be barricaded to keep animals away from the crops. Plant your garden where it will receive appropriate sun. Vegetables can be grown in raised beds, containers, or traditional gardens.

Composting Locate compost bins close to the kitchen but away from viewing and entertaining areas. Compost bins are an excellent means of recycling food scraps and yard clippings for later use in your garden.

Storage Determine storage needs for landscaping equipment, gardening tools, sports equipment and seasonal furniture. Consider electrical needs when designing storage structures. You can finish and paint these structures to suit the landscape theme.

Expanding the House Decks and patios can be attached to the house to extend the indoor living area or located as separate outdoor rooms. A small deck in the garden can add another functional area to view and enjoy your landscape.

PRACTICAL ELEMENTS

All of the practical necessities of outdoor living need to be integrated into the landscape design. Storage sheds and garbage cans are examples of important functional objects that must not be left off the wish list or out of the landscape plan. Few of these features are attractive in their own right, but with proper planning they can be made to fit in well.

Utilitarian requirements, including storage sheds for gardening equipment, compost bins, pool pumps, garbage cans and clotheslines, should be situated for convenience and away from view lines. Clustering these items around one all-purpose service area adjoining the house is the best way to avoid having eyesores in the middle of the landscape. If the service area cannot be placed completely out of sight, it can be disguised. Vine-covered fences, trellises and arbors will conceal less attractive features of the landscape.

Utilities are another practical consideration that cannot be forgotten in your plans. Irrigation and lighting require power and plumbing. Identify the location of electrical receptacles and hose bibs. To save money, use existing outlets rather than installing new ones. Be sure there is electricity available for pumps and work areas. Find out if water lines reach the places needing irrigation and if there is natural gas available for the barbecue. Avoid placing features requiring utilities where lines will have to be installed under existing driveways or patios.

UNDERSTANDING CLIMATE FACTORS

The prevailing weather patterns, the microclimate created by the local terrain and the orientation of the lot must all be considered when planning use areas. Growing conditions and appropriate outdoor activities vary dramatically from one corner of the property to another.

Exposure Wind and rains driven from one direction can be blocked by tall trees, garden walls and other windscreens.

Drainage Take into account natural drainage. Interrupting this flow can cause flooding into your house or a neighboring property.

Sunlight Track variations in sunlight and shadow through the seasons to determine locations for various activities and plants.

Type of Soil Native soil that is acid or alkaline, too dense or too light for some plants, must be corrected.

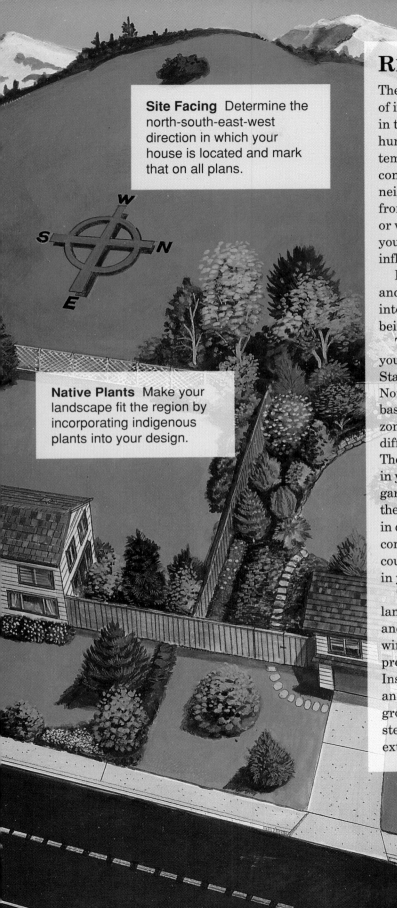

Site Facing Determine the north-south-east-west direction in which your house is located and mark that on all plans.

Native Plants Make your landscape fit the region by incorporating indigenous plants into your design.

REGIONAL DIFFERENCES

The climate surrounding your house consists of its prevailing weather conditions, described in terms of the annual precipitation, humidity, winds and average range of temperatures. Within large regions, local conditions create *microclimates*, so that any neighborhood may feel very different effects from altitude, site orientation, sun and shade or wind chill. The orientation and slope of your lot also creates microclimate effects that influence plant selection and area use.

Every region also has a history of land use and architecture. This tradition translates into landscape themes that are recognized as being suited to the area.

The region affects the type of plants that you can install in your landscape. The United States Department of Agriculture has divided North America into 11 plant hardiness zones based on minimum temperatures within the zone. However, your microclimate may be different from that of the average for the zone. The best way to see the plants that will do well in your yard is to take a look at nearby gardens to see which plants are thriving and then duplicate those conditions in your yard. If in doubt about which plants are suitable, consult a local nursery or your agricultural county extension agent about the conditions in your area.

There are ways to modify the existing landscape to improve growing conditions and the appearance of the terrain. Plant windscreens of tall evergreens to block prevailing winds and prevent wind erosion. Install drainage fields to dry out low spots and stabilize very wet soil. Use grasses or groundcover to hold the soil together on steep slopes or build retaining walls to extend the useful area of the yard.

EVALUATING THE SITE

Before you can plan the new landscape, you must determine exactly what you have now. Spend time viewing the yard from the house, dreaming of what you'd rather be seeing. Walk around outside with an eye for ways to improve your lot.

Boundary Markers Check survey stakes or fences against the dimensions of the lot on the property papers.

Service Entrance The service area usually includes utility boxes and garbage cans.

Views Check views from various rooms of the house to the yard and views from the yard to the greater landscape.

Noise Street and neighbor noises should be considered when placing activity areas in your yard.

Utilities Look for electrical receptacles and hose bibs around the house, which indicate power and water sources.

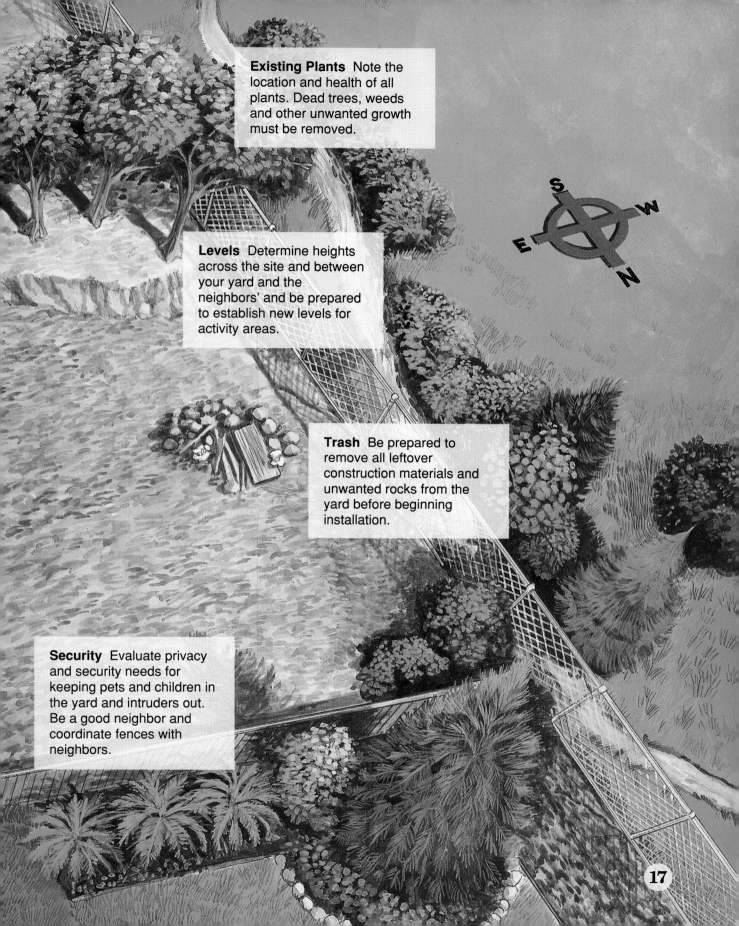

Existing Plants Note the location and health of all plants. Dead trees, weeds and other unwanted growth must be removed.

Levels Determine heights across the site and between your yard and the neighbors' and be prepared to establish new levels for activity areas.

Trash Be prepared to remove all leftover construction materials and unwanted rocks from the yard before beginning installation.

Security Evaluate privacy and security needs for keeping pets and children in the yard and intruders out. Be a good neighbor and coordinate fences with neighbors.

PUTTING IDEAS ON PAPER

DRAWING A BASE PLAN

Begin to visualize a design for your landscape by drawing a base plan showing the exact property lines, the size and location of the house and other buildings, any changes in levels that occur on the property and the location of utilities and existing features.

The house and landscape depicted on pgs. 16–17, shown before any work has been done, is used as the sample throughout this series of drawings.

Using stakes to mark the corners of the lot, walk off the perimeter of the property carrying a 100 foot tape. Then measure and write down the distances between the major structures, noting their placement relative to a single point of reference.

Situate the house, existing decks, porches, patios and outbuildings on the base plan, accurately showing their measured dimensions and the direction they face.

To make it easier to draw your garden plan, use graph or grid paper, which has horizontal and vertical ruled lines. These lines form squares, usually with either four, five, eight, or ten little squares to each inch. Assume that each little square will equal one foot of actual measurement in your garden; the scale of your drawing will then be one inch equals four, five, eight or ten feet. If your yard is very small, four or five feet to the inch may be the right scale to use. If you have a really large lot, you may have to make each little square equal two feet, so that one inch will equal 16 or 20 feet, in order to get the entire drawing on one sheet of paper. Use the same scale for all drawings—base plan, bubble diagrams, hardscape plan, planting plan and final landscape plan.

Gather drawing tools and establish an out-of-the-way area in which to draw your landscape plans. The process will take some time, and it is better not to have to move the delicate drawings too often. Purchase graph paper, tracing paper, two or three colors of pencils, an eraser, drafting tape, a triangle, a T-square, a straightedge and a landscape template to use throughout the process. Make sure there is good light available and you have a comfortable chair in which to sit as you may find you'll want to work for hours at a time.

CAUTION

Check local codes, covenants and restrictions before finalizing the design.

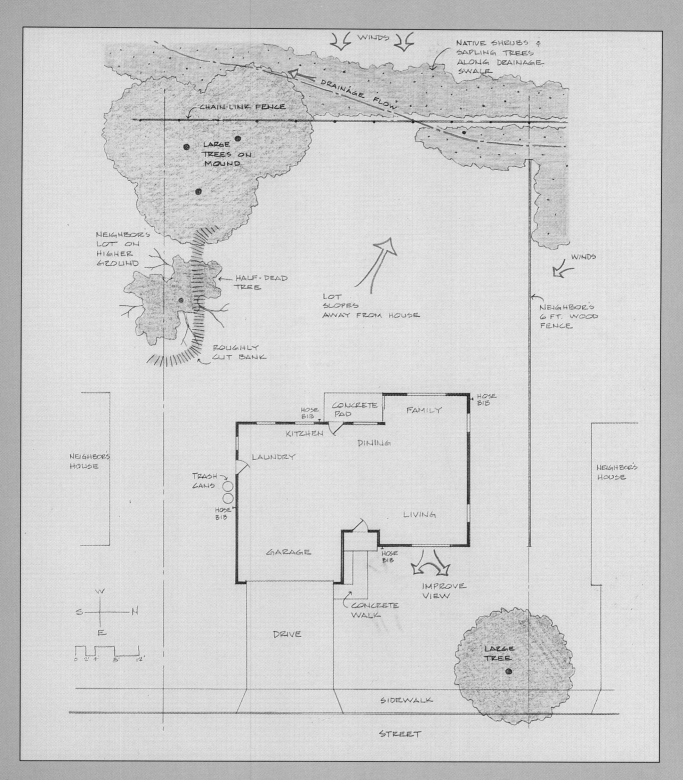

WINDS

NATIVE SHRUBS &
SAPLING TREES
ALONG DRAINAGE
SWALE

DRAINAGE FLOW

CHAIN-LINK FENCE

LARGE
TREES ON
MOUND

NEIGHBOR'S
LOT ON
HIGHER
GROUND

HALF-DEAD
TREE

WINDS

NEIGHBOR'S
6 FT. WOOD
FENCE

LOT
SLOPES
AWAY FROM HOUSE

ROUGHLY
CUT BANK

CONCRETE
PAD

HOSE
BIB

FAMILY

HOSE
BIB

KITCHEN

DINING

NEIGHBOR'S
HOUSE

LAUNDRY

TRASH
CANS

NEIGHBOR'S
HOUSE

HOSE
BIB

LIVING

GARAGE

HOSE
BIB

IMPROVE
VIEW

CONCRETE
WALK

W
S ─┼─ N
E

0 2' 4'   8'   12'

DRIVE

LARGE
TREE

SIDEWALK

STREET

19

CREATING A BUBBLE DIAGRAM

Make several photocopies or tracings of the base plan and use them to create bubble diagrams. Drawing bubble diagrams allows you to visualize the landscape as an interlocking system of activity areas—entertaining, gardening, play areas—defined by walls, fences or edgings and connected by pathways, entrances and steps. By drawing a series of different bubble diagrams, you will get a good idea of how much space different activities need and how well different arrangements work.

Draw the bubble diagram using the wish list as your guide and keeping in mind the principles of design and your landscape theme. Draw rough outlines of the areas in terms of their passive or active uses. Buffer zones and open spaces should alternate with heavy traffic and high-activity areas. Show entrances and pathways with arrows; indicate important views and shady or sunny spaces. Except where they border on existing features, the bubbles can be rough estimates of the area relationships. This is the problem-solving stage of the design process, in which such questions as how to screen one area from another should be raised and answered.

Once you've completed one bubble diagram, take another copy of the base plan and make a second and third bubble plan. Look at how the activity areas relate to each other, and where the transition from one space to another occurs. Play with various ideas, then line them up and compare them. One will emerge as the plan that best suits the space, fulfills the desires on the wish list and works with the landscape theme.

SAMPLE WISH LIST

Use your wish list while working on your bubble drawings. This wish list, written for the house featured in the sample drawings, uses typical categories.

Site Corrections
Fencing backyard for security, privacy, dog enclosure
Eliminating dead tree
Softening back chain-link fence
Accomodating property grade with that of southern neighbor
Covering garbage/storage area
Shading kitchen from western exposure in afternoons
Making front entrance more welcoming
Establishing a view from living room

Desired Maintenance Level
30 percent low-maintenance
50 percent medium-maintenance
20 percent high-maintenance

Desired Activities
Entertaining near kitchen/dining room
Toddler's play area
Playing lawn games
Sitting quietly/contemplation area
Hanging out some laundry
Swimming in a pool
Attracting animals

Gardening Areas
Vegetable/herb garden
Cutting flower garden
Year-round greenery
Seasonal color
Shade trees

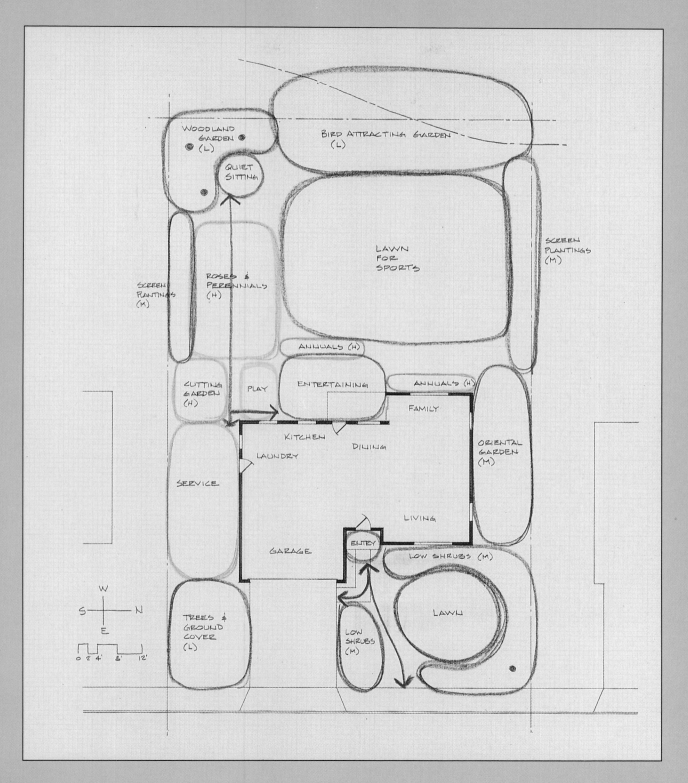

WOODLAND
GARDEN
(L)

BIRD ATTRACTING GARDEN
(L)

QUIET
SITTING

SCREEN
PLANTINGS
(M)

LAWN
FOR
SPORTS

ROSES &
PERENNIALS
(H)

SCREEN
PLANTINGS
(M)

ANNUALS (H)

CUTTING
GARDEN
(H)

PLAY

ENTERTAINING

ANNUALS (H)

FAMILY

KITCHEN

DINING

ORIENTAL
GARDEN
(M)

LAUNDRY

SERVICE

LIVING

GARAGE

ENTRY

LOW SHRUBS (M)

W
S   N
E

LAWN

TREES &
GROUND
COVER
(L)

LOW
SHRUBS
(M)

0 2 4'   8'   12'

21

SCALING THE PLAN

THE HARDSCAPE PLAN

Once you have determined the bubble diagram that best suits your needs, you need to draw a detailed, accurate version of the hardscape features shown in their correct size and relationship.

Take a clean copy of the base plan and draw the new hardscape features onto it (or on a tracing paper overlay of the base plan).

Every hardscape structure—buildings, paths, patios, decks, edgings, fences, utility areas and irrigation and light fixtures—must be drawn to exact size. Indicate paving and building materials. A simple reference table can take the place of a realistic drawing of the material itself. Indicate surface types with letters (A for asphalt, B for bark and so on or with different drawing patterns for different surface materials). If levels will be changed in construction, indicate the existing and desired topographical changes. Include the directional indicator and the scale used.

If your freehand drawing is poor, use a landscape template, available at art stores or drafting supply shops, to draw in various elements. Remember to match the scale of the template to the scale of the drawing.

Before you complete the hardscape plan, make sure that the sizes meet minimum requirements, that desired views have been obtained and that the orientation of major features is proper.

GUIDE TO SIZES

Every functional structure in the landscape has minimum size requirements, below which they should not be built.

Paths

A path for one person needs to be 24–30 inches wide. For two people, a primary walk needs to be four to six feet wide, a secondary walk three feet wide.

Fences and Gates

Build security fences at least six feet high. Build all fences either below or above eye level. Build gates three feet wide. Gates wider than four feet may require supports. Gates for vehicles must be ten feet wide.

Play Areas

Spas can be scaled to fit the available space. However, to be worthwhile, a swimming pool should be at least 25 feet long and six feet wide.

Basketball courts can be built around a garage entrance and driveway, allowing for a ten foot high hoop. There's no point in building a tennis court to less than regulation size.

The size of children's play areas is more flexible; a four feet by four feet sandbox is suitable for toddlers.

Driveways

A one-car garage in a suburban area requires a driveway 12–14 feet wide, centered on the door. Two-car garages must have a driveway 18 feet wide; curved drives should be 14–18 feet wide. Parking spaces should be nine feet wide and 18 feet long at a minimum.

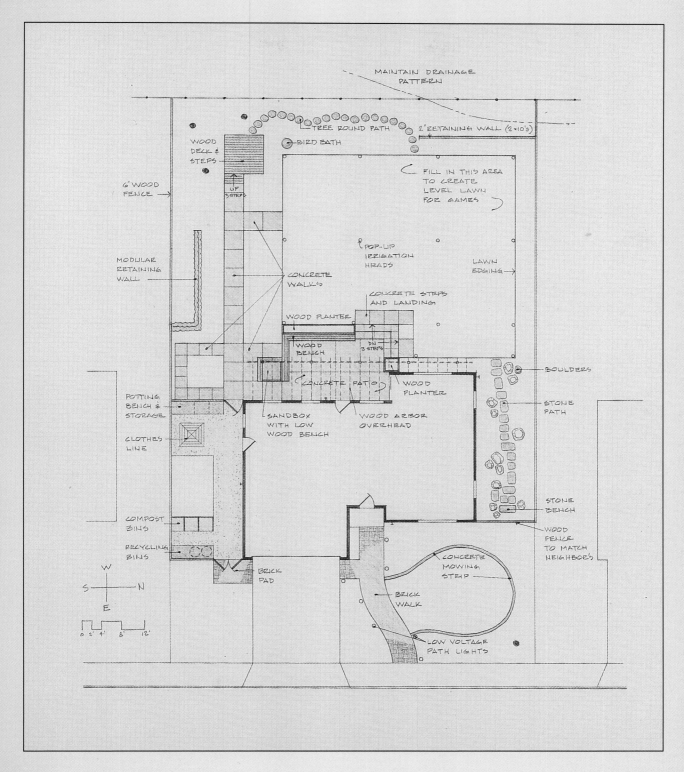

MAINTAIN DRAINAGE
PATTERN

TREE ROUND PATH

2' RETAINING WALL (2 x 10's)

BIRD BATH

WOOD
DECK &
STEPS

FILL IN THIS AREA
TO CREATE
LEVEL LAWN
FOR GAMES

6' WOOD
FENCE

UP
3 STEPS

POP-UP
IRRIGATION
HEADS

LAWN
EDGING

MODULAR
RETAINING
WALL

CONCRETE
WALKS

CONCRETE STEPS
AND LANDING

WOOD PLANTER

WOOD
BENCH

DN
3 STEPS

BOULDERS

CONCRETE PATIO

WOOD
PLANTER

STONE
PATH

POTTING
BENCH &
STORAGE

SANDBOX
WITH LOW
WOOD BENCH

WOOD ARBOR
OVERHEAD

CLOTHES
LINE

STONE
BENCH

COMPOST
BINS

WOOD
FENCE
TO MATCH
NEIGHBOR'S

RECYCLING
BINS

W

S   N

E

CONCRETE
MOWING
STRIP

BRICK
PAD

BRICK
WALK

0 2' 4'   8'   12'

LOW VOLTAGE
PATH LIGHTS

FINALIZING THE PLAN

PLANTING DESIGN

Planting design combines beauty and practicality. Every plant has a unique form, size, color and texture. The successful composition is based on combining these principles of design (see pg. 7) with plants that are suitable to your climate (see pgs. 14–15) using the practical guidelines presented here.

Plants solve many site problems. Most obviously, use plants as screens to hide poor views, or install a beautiful specimen plant to establish a focal point in the landscape. Plants can also be used to soften built structures. For example, planting vines to grow on a stark chain link fence softens it and makes it look less institutional.

Use plants to direct traffic. Shrubs planted as hedges form barriers between activity areas, annuals as edgings define shapes in the garden, and small trees control movement through the yard.

Plants are effective for wind reduction, reducing wind over a distance five times their height. For a windbreak, plan a double row of trees with shorter shrubs beneath.

Shade trees reduce the temperature of the area beneath them by 10°F. Plants can also reduce home heating and cooling costs. Deciduous trees near windows will block the summer sun yet allow winter sun to warm the house.

Install groundcovers and grasses on hillsides and slopes to reduce erosion. The closer the spacing, the better the control.

Plants also reduce noise to some degree. Plant a buffer of trees and shrubs between the source of the noise and your yard to decrease sound levels.

FINAL PLAN

The final plan is a detailed drawing that shows all the landscape design elements from a fixed overhead perspective. Assemble the final drawing by adding the planting design to the hardscape plan.

On the bubble diagram, you determined the general planting areas. Now each area must be filled with suitable plants.

Arrange the specimens within each of the major plant groups: conifer and deciduous trees, shrubs, groundcovers and grasses, vines and climbers and annual and perennial bedding plants. Draw the locations of the individual plants onto the hardscape plan or on a separate overlay. Show the planting point as a dot and the extension of foilage, called the "drip line," as a circle. Draw existing elements, hardscape elements and greenscape elements in different colors to make them distinctive on the final plan.

Use the final plan for estimating and purchasing materials and for planning and obtaining permits for construction projects. Bring a copy of the plan along when purchasing plants or discussing growing conditions at your local nursery or garden supply store. The final plan serves as a long-term guide for the most effective installation of plants and features over the life of the landscape.

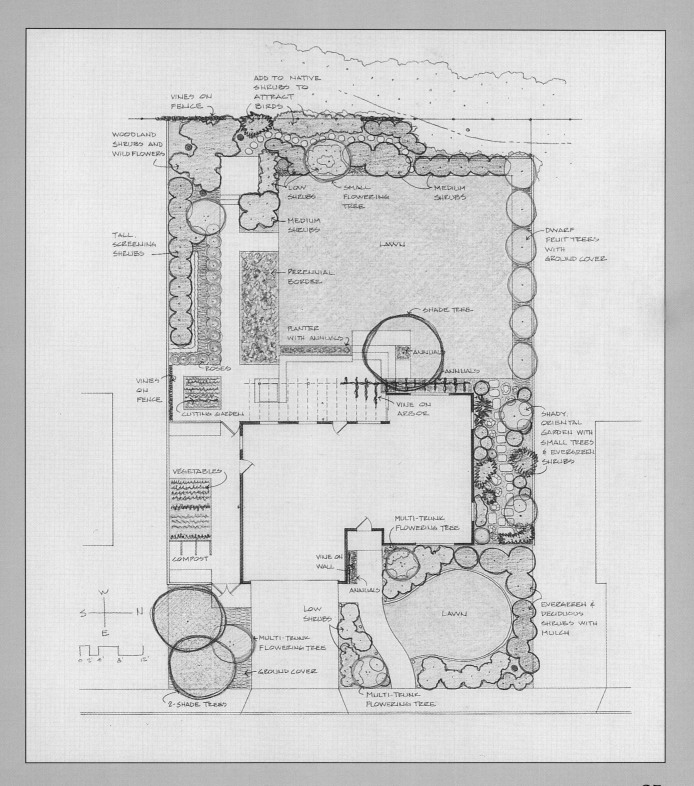

VINES ON FENCE

ADD TO NATIVE SHRUBS TO ATTRACT BIRDS

WOODLAND SHRUBS AND WILD FLOWERS

LOW SHRUBS

SMALL FLOWERING TREE

MEDIUM SHRUBS

MEDIUM SHRUBS

TALL, SCREENING SHRUBS

LAWN

DWARF FRUIT TREES WITH GROUND COVER

PERENNIAL BORDER

SHADE TREE

PLANTER WITH ANNUALS

ANNUALS

ANNUALS

ROSES

VINES ON FENCE

VINE ON ARBOR

CUTTING GARDEN

SHADY, ORIENTAL GARDEN WITH SMALL TREES & EVERGREEN SHRUBS

VEGETABLES

MULTI-TRUNK FLOWERING TREE

COMPOST

VINE ON WALL

ANNUALS

W N S E

LOW SHRUBS

LAWN

EVERGREEN & DECIDUOUS SHRUBS WITH MULCH

MULTI-TRUNK FLOWERING TREE

GROUND COVER

0 2' 4'   8'   12'

2-SHADE TREES

MULTI-TRUNK FLOWERING TREE

BRINGING THE PLAN TO LIFE

The final plan on the previous page is brought to life after the construction of the hardscape and the installation of the greenscape, shown here approximately three years after completion.

26

KEY TO DRAWING

Note the number of items on the home-owner's wish list (see pg. 20) that have been realized in this landscape design.

1. A lighted path from the sidewalk to the house welcomes visitors. The brick matches the brick detailing on the house, providing harmony in the design.

2. Tucked away at the side of the house, the service area serves garbage, recycling, composting, vegetable gardening, clothesline and storage needs.

3. A simple wood fence now encloses the yard. A gate fronting the service area provides access. Fence design and installation were coordinated with neighbors.

4. The dead tree was removed and a modular retaining wall installed to hold back the higher level of the neighboring yard.

5. A detached deck becomes a quiet spot for adults to relax while viewing children's activities on the lawn and in the sandbox.

6. Expanding the patio and adding benches provide space for entertaining. The arbor shades the west side of the house and the sandbox.

7. A large lawn with an installed irrigation system is a perfect expanse for lawn games. Someday it may be replaced with a swimming pool when finances allow and the children are older. A deciduous tree shades the patio.

8. The view is emphasized by native plants that visually link the yard to the larger landscape. Vines soften the chain link fence. Leaving this area undisturbed allows natural drainage to flow.

9. A line of dwarf fruit trees planted along the fence reduces prevailing winds and buffers noise from the neighbor's yard.

10. The small-space garden can be seen from the living and family rooms. It is low-maintenance with an Oriental theme to match the interior design.

ENVISIONING THE MATURE LANDSCAPE

LOOKING AHEAD

After the landscape design has been completed but before the installation, spend some time visualizing what the mature landscape will look like. After five years or so, the size and shape of the greenscape will have changed considerably. The shadows created by growing shrubs and trees will encourage the appearance of shade-loving plants in their vicinity; open areas will see native plants reappear and take over unless you mount a campaign to remove them.

Proper plant selection will reduce the amount of maintenance, however, a certain amount of upkeep is always necessary. Trees and shrubs have to be pruned or removed if they outgrow their location. Overhanging limbs and branches and luxuriant foliage have to be trimmed to protect the house and other structures from damage. Expanding root systems have to be checked for potential damage to underground pipes, cables and sewer lines.

Hardscape elements also need annual protection and eventual replacement. Wood structures must be sealed against water damage. Concrete surfaces must be inspected for cracks and repaired. Brick and stone surfaces must be regrouted occasionally.

Changes in your life-style will also occur. For example, the space for a toddler's sandbox may be better used for a swing set for elementary-school-aged children and as a spa when the children reach high school. As your life-style needs change over the years, adjust the landscape elements accordingly.

28

After One Year

After Five Years

Growth in the Landscape Plan the spacing
of trees, shrubs and other plants to suit their
full size at maturity. Use a plant guide to
figure the height, volume and general shape
of larger greenscape elements at the time of
planting, after one year and after five years.

29

GATHERING TOOLS AND EQUIPMENT

LANDSCAPING EQUIPMENT

Moving large amounts of soil requires heavy equipment such as backhoes, front end loaders, crawlers and heavy drilling rigs for wells and foundation postholes. Hire experienced operators for these bigger jobs.

Landscape contractors, building contractors and individual operators can provide these services. Get references and consult with the contractor to confirm the exact job, schedule and payment procedure before he or she begins work.

For smaller jobs, consider renting lighter equipment and doing the work yourself. Power rotary tillers, fence posthole drillers, small front loaders, portable concrete mixers and myriad other pieces of equipment are available for rent. Check the telephone directory for agencies near you. Renting rather than buying equipment eliminates maintenance and storage problems. The cost for a one-time operation is usually reasonable.

If you will be doing a lot of work over a long period of time, buying good equipment can be a cost-effective investment. Be sure to learn how to operate all power equipment before using it. Look into the availability of parts and service in your area for any landscaping equipment you buy, and think about where you will store it when it is not in use.

Garden Rake

Power Mower

Drop Spreader

Pitchfork

Cultivator

Weed Trimmer

GARDENING TOOLS

Hose and Soaker

Pruning Saw

You'll need a good set of gardening tools for installing and maintaining the landscape. A full set of basic gardening tools includes rakes, shovels and hoes for working the soil; clippers, shears and saws for pruning trees and shrubs; a trowel and cultivator for vegetable and flower gardening; a drop spreader, power mower and weed trimmer for lawn maintenance; a wheelbarrow for moving compost, fertilizer and debris; and a heavy push broom for sweeping paths and decks. Everyone helping with gardening chores needs quality work gloves, sturdy shoes and sun protection when working outside.

A sturdy, well-made tool will reward the owner with a lifetime of service; don't try to save money by purchasing tools with flimsy handles or poor construction. Try out hand tools for feel and fit and buy only products that come with a warranty and return rights, in case they prove defective.

Store gardening tools in a dry, secure toolshed located near the garden work area. After every use, clean the tools well to prevent rust and return them to their proper location. Be sure to wipe and oil all iron and steel surfaces when putting tools away for any length of time, and pick loose tools up off the floor or ground for safety.

Storage racks, hangers or modular wall systems are useful for organizing and displaying hand tools; quick, convenient access will save many hours of searching for small, easy-to-misplace items. A worker is only as good as his tools—keep them clean, sharp and handy.

Rotary Tiller

Wheelbarrow

Garden Shovel

Garden Hoe

SOLVING DRAINAGE PROBLEMS

SOILS AND SLOPES

Drainage problems are usually easy to spot: either water flows too quickly across the yard, removing topsoil, or surface water pools during rains and the ground is waterlogged for days afterward. These problems are caused by too severe a slope and poor soil drainage.

The slope of a terrain is the difference in elevation between any two points of rising or falling ground (five to one equals a rise of one foot for every five feet). To even the slope, cut, fill and level the problem area. To direct surface water away from foundations, driveways and sidewalks, build up earthen mounds on stable ground and guide the flow of surface water around them and toward established drainage channels. Established channels include creeks, storm drains and dry wells. If necessary, install drainage systems in low areas where water accumulates.

Well-drained, fertile topsoil over a stable but permeable layer of subsoil is best for growing landscape plants. A simple drainage test will reveal if the soil drains properly. Dig a hole one foot across and two feet deep and fill it to the brim with water during a dry spell. If the water takes more than 15 or less than five minutes to drain completely, the soil needs improvement. Sandy, loose soils drain too quickly, while heavy clay soils become waterlogged and cause surface water to run off without penetrating to root systems. Loose soil is more prone to erosion than planted areas. By channeling excess surface water into drainage channels, you will protect loose earth until plants are established enough to knit together.

Leveling

First Unload fill soil next to area to be leveled. Cut down high spots.

Next Test level with sighting equipment; add changes to slopes on base plan.

Last Move earth to fill in low spots and level off remaining high spots.

Garden Drainage

First Mark off low area with garden lime or stake and string, and design drain line system to follow length of low area to drainage channel. For a large area of poor drainage, several parallel drain lines may be needed.

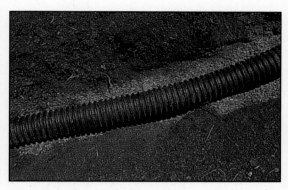

Third Lay 4 in. diameter plastic drainage pipe with perforation holes facing down on top of the gravel in each trench.

Then Dig trench 16–24 in. deep, centered on the lowest spot. Slope each trench 3–4 in. deeper for each 100 ft. of length heading toward the drainage channel. Fill the base of each trench with 2–3 in. of coarse, crushed gravel.

Last Cover pipe with a 4 in. layer of gravel and tamp down surface. Fill the rest of the trench with soil and amendments as required for installing plants.

CHOOSING PAVING MATERIALS

Lay out the shape of paths in accordance with design principles and the widths according to safety guidelines. Choose paving materials to match your theme and budget, considering the costs over the lifetime of the landscape.

Concrete Concrete walks are level, skid-proof surfaces suitable for high-traffic areas. Slabs can be textured or colored to suit any landscape theme.

Brick Bricks go well with a range of landscape styles from Traditional American to Cottage to Moorish. Use severe weather (SW) grade bricks.

Review the principles of design when determining the shape of paths. They can direct axis, provide rhythm, determine scale and divide spaces. The paving materials provide color and texture.

Wood Sawed logs, timbers and shredded or chipped wood all create attractive garden floors, good for natural themes. Solid wood planks and above-ground decking are easier to clean up but take more work to construct.

Crushed Stone Gravel pathways are particularly well suited to Traditional American and Oriental landscapes. Use coarse gravel, crushed stone or pea gravel for paths with drainage problems. Wood or metal edgings or concrete mowing string along gravel paths will greatly reduce maintenance work.

PATHS AND STEPS

Paths and steps perform two important functions in the landscape. They create a comfortable physical and psychological transition from one activity area to another, and they provide access to the house, the yard and plants needing maintenance work.

A smooth, inviting and well-lit path provides a sense of security and well-being for the house entrance. For safety and utility, grade and level all main paths and leave a buffer area along the edges, so two people can stroll side-by-side without feeling hemmed in. Use durable, skid-proof materials in paved areas that are frequently damp and slippery. Concrete, asphalt and paving blocks create uniform, stable surfaces for moderate prices. Brick, slate and flagstone are more expensive but may be just the material needed to fit your landscape theme. Natural materials such as shredded bark, river pebbles and fieldstone are less expensive, less durable, but attractive alternatives.

Curved paths are more visually appealing than straight ones. Curves create a sense of mystery that causes people to want to continue forward. Wind the path around steep slopes or rocky surfaces and through natural entryways and passages to provide ever-changing garden views, always avoiding sharp turns or abrupt endings.

Use steps or stairways to connect levels within the yard. Make sure the steps are wide, even and uniform in size. Use the standard ratio of rise-to-run for outdoor steps, with two times the riser height plus one tread length equaling 26 inches, the stride of an average adult. For example, if the riser is five inches high, the tread should be 16 inches wide ($5 \times 2 = 10 + 16 = 26$). Break up long runs with landings for resting or viewing the landscape. Build steps wider than paths to avoid a cramped feeling.

INSTALLING PAVING MATERIALS

Use the same methods for installing paving materials on paths and patios. Exercise caution when moving heavy materials. As with most construction projects, you'll find installing paving materials is much easier when done with a helper.

Installing an intricate pattern of bricks or irregularly shaped materials such as these flagstones requires that you first set out a dry run—a practice installation—to find the best fit.

Setting Brick on Sand

First Lay out a border around area with stakes and string. Dig bed 4 in. deep for bricks and sand (deeper if gravel drainage bed is required).

Next Dig a trench 4 in. deeper around the perimeter for upright edging bricks. Spread 2 in. of sand. Wet and roll or firmly tamp the base, using a board.

Last Set bricks in the desired pattern, tapping into place with rubber mallet. Use 4 ft. mason's level to align and level surfaces. Trim bricks to fit using a mason's hammer.

Building a Gravel Path

First Lay out the walkway using stakes and string. Dig a 2 in. deep trench with square sides the length of the path. Install strip edging.

Next Fill with gravel 3/8–5/8 in. size to just below edging.

Last Smooth, tamp and level using a bow rake.

PLANNING PATIOS AND DECKS

Patios are hard-surfaced activity areas laid at ground level. Decks are raised surfaces, which can be attached to the house or not. Plan the size of patios and decks in scale with the house and yard.

CONCRETE SLAB PATIO
A poured concrete patio provides a handsome, hard-wearing surface for work or play. The concrete can be given a smooth, textured or stamped pattern finish.

CONCRETE FACTS

Concrete is a rugged, durable building material used for a variety of elements in the landscape. Installation methods are the same for all projects, whether paths, patios or mowing strips.

Concrete is a mix of roughly one part cement, two parts sand and four parts gravel. Small amounts can be mixed by hand on site.

Larger quantities, measured in cubic yards, should be purchased from ready-mix firms. Ready-mixed concrete delivered to the site must be unloaded in a short period of time. The site must be completely prepared, laid out and leveled, and the forms built before the concrete arrives. The amount of concrete to be ordered varies according to its paste, or water-cement ratio; higher ratios of water to cement result in a weaker paste suitable for light uses. The ready-mix firm will figure the amount of concrete you need based on the square footage to be covered.

Installing concrete is not a one-person job; if you choose to do it yourself, be sure helpers are available and that someone on your crew has experience. Consider beginning with a smaller project, such as a mowing strip (see pgs. 56–57), to learn the tricks of pouring and finishing concrete.

BUILDING DECKS

A simple detached, ground-level, wooden deck, such as the one described here, creates a level activity area anywhere in the yard. Building an attached deck, which requires bolting a ledger to the house, is a more ambitious project.

CAUTION

Always use pressure-treated or rot-resistant wood and galvanized nails and screws for decks.

Building a Simple Detached Deck

First Measure the area of the deck from the dimensions on the hardscape plan. The deck will be built on a grid supported by piers. Measure the position of the piers 4 ft. on center apart and mark them with stakes and string.

Fourth For ground-level decks, toenail beams to nailer blocks in piers. For above-ground decks, attach posts to nailer blocks in piers; correct differences in ground height by cutting tops of posts to same level and attach beams to posts.

Seventh Fit joists into hangers to form a 4 x 4 ft. grid. Level and support the completed grid with rot-resistant shims placed between joists and beams, as needed.

Then Using a post-hole digger or shovel, dig holes for support piers 2 ft. deep by 2 ft. square. In cold climates dig below frost line.

Fifth Using a carpenter's level, check to see that each post and beam is level (even horizontally) and plumb (even vertically).

Next Nail or screw decking boards across joists and beams, leaving 1/8 in. gaps between boards. Trim edges of decking boards, as needed.

Third Fill holes with mixed concrete to within 1/2 ft. of surface to form footings. Let concrete set slightly; place precast piers on footings.

Sixth Attach hangers to sides of beams, using galvanized nails or screws.

Last For a finished appearance, nail fascia boards around outside, covering the edges of the decking boards.

PLANNING OUTDOOR WALLS

FORMING BOUNDARIES

Landscape boundaries include fences, garden walls and hedges. They enclose the yard, separate activity areas, obscure or frame views and serve as a backdrop for plants.

Boundaries have a significant impact on the look and feel of the design. Choose materials to match the landscape theme and to coordinate with your house and neighboring boundaries. Plan their height, width and direction in accordance with the principles of scale and line, and the materials based on the principles of color and texture.

Fences can be made of wood or metal. Designs vary, but all are made of the same components: posts, rails and infill. Build fences above or below the line of sight, not at eye level. Low fences are mainly decorative. For privacy, build fences higher than five feet high.

Garden walls can be either retaining or freestanding structures. Either type can be made of mortared or unmortared brick, stone or precast concrete, railroad ties or timbers. Freestanding walls serve mainly to separate different areas. All garden walls higher than three feet should be engineered by a professional. Make sure that every wall has solid footings and good drainage.

Living hedges are formed by planting shrubs or trees close to each other and allowing the branches to grow together. Clever pruning can turn a functional hedge into a work of topiary art, forming a focal point in the landscape. Because hedges will take some time to grow to the planned height, consider installing a temporary fence—lattice is a good material for this option—until the shrubs have grown tall enough to form the desired boundary.

Lattice Fence Lattice panels and louvers create a partial screen while letting air and light into the garden. Alternating patterns of shade and sun give visual texture to the interior. Lattice is effective for tall fences because its open feel will not become overpowering.

Picket Fence The low white picket fence defines the borders of the garden in the Traditional American style but allows the passerby to see the landscape within. Picket fences can be built at any height and left natural, stained or painted a color other than white for different effects.

Stone Wall The mass and texture of a stone wall brings a sense of solidity to the activity area it encloses. Stone walls are often mortared, but natural stone walls can also be built by fitting stones together carefully. This is an excellent use of stones found on the property.

Hedge Evergreen shrubs are most commonly used for hedges. There are 3 basic hedge heights: low, less than 12 in., for bordering beds; medium, up to 6 ft., for property boundaries; and high, over 6 ft., for controlling wind and blocking views. Cacti and roses also make effective hedges because their thorns detour animals and intruders.

Cost Considerations

The cost of outdoor wall construction depends on the materials and on the amount of labor involved. You will almost always save money on materials by purchasing goods produced locally.

The least expensive garden wall material is railroad ties, followed by cinder block and concrete block. Cast blocks are most commonly found in a standard $8 \times 8 \times 16$ inch size. Concrete blocks of this dimension will weigh about five pounds, lighter cinder block slightly less, and their costs vary accordingly. More attractive 12×12 inch open-work blocks cost a little more than cement block, but they are lighter, faster to build with and nicer looking. For ease of construction, consider mortarless modular walls of precast concrete (see pgs. 46–47).

Mortared brick is a handsome, durable wall material, but the higher cost and structural limitations of brick must be taken into account. A single-width wall needs fifty bricks per square yard of wall, and the double-brick construction needed to build over three feet high needs twice as many. Used bricks are preferred for their weathered appearance and can sometimes be found at demolition sites or dumps at a considerable savings over new brick prices.

Stone walls are built with *rubble*, rough stone of varied dimensions, or *ashlar*, flat quarried stone with only minor irregularities. These materials are the most expensive, unless you happen to have a ready supply of suitable rock in your yard. The stones must be individually fit, which takes patience, skill and time. Building costs can be quite high.

43

BUILDING FENCES

Although wooden fences can be designed in a variety of styles, the building methods for all are basically the same. For construction of a simple, solid board fence, use quickset dry mortar mix (one bag per posthole), galvanized three inch nails, and precut fence boards for the inlay.

A well-built fence will provide privacy, define the boundary and look attractive on both sides. Use fir, pine, redwood or any other locally available species of exterior-grade, rot-resistant or pressure-treated lumber.

Building Fences

First Lay out end and corner points of fence. Space posts 6–8 ft. apart on center. Dig postholes at least 2 ft. deep, or below frost line. Nail bracing arms on 2 ground stakes 3 ft. from end post.

Then Set end post in hole, plumb on two sides with level. Set upright with braces nailed loosely to post. Check alignment of posts and level again.

Third Pour quickset concrete mix into hole around post up to ground level, pour in water and stir until cement is of uniform consistency. Repeat for all corner and end posts; check alignment.

Fourth Adjust intermediate posts with alignment string at top and bottom, so post faces are in flat line. Plumb posts, adjust braces and pour quickset concrete mix into holes, one at a time.

Next Allow concrete to set overnight. Join rails to posts. Use lap joints on top rails, butt joints on bottom rails.

Last Nail on siding boards. Use a spacer board to insure uniform gap between siding boards.

Installing Gates

First Measure space between level gateposts at top and at bottom for frame size. Leave 1 in. gaps on both sides for hinges and clearance. Using T-square to keep rails at right angles, nail frame together.

Next Attach diagonal brace to frame at inside corners using 2 1/2 in. wood screws through both horizontal and vertical rails. Attach boards starting at hinge side, using spacer for uniform distance between boards.

Third Using galvanized hardware, attach hinges to gatepost. Prop gate in place and attach hinges to frame. Attach latch to gate and frame using 1 1/2 in. wood screws or bolts.

BUILDING GARDEN WALLS

Retaining walls up to three feet in height can be built by the homeowner. Heavy soils or steeply rising slopes behind the wall require sturdier construction methods.

Building a natural stone wall is an art. The stones can be dry-fit or mortared. All garden walls must have a gravel backfill and drainage holes to carry run-off water from the soil behind them.

Building Modular Walls

First Dig a shallow trench to the depth and width of the modules; walls 3 ft. and lower can be set on firm, level soil.

Fourth Backfill behind each new course of modules with granular fill (gravel, pea rock) for drainage.

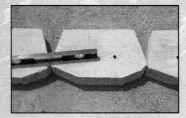

Then Install base course, placing modules side by side with hollow side down. Check level and adjust, if necessary.

Next Place second and succeeding courses in a running bond pattern, bridging two modules below with each new module.

Third If locking pins are used, insert pins into holes on top of modules to position the next layer of modules.

Last Install a course of cap units (cast without pinholes in top) to complete wall. Cement cap layer in place for added security.

PLANNING IRRIGATION

ANALYZING WATER NEEDS

Assess your overall water usage when deciding irrigation needs. Systems range from manual irrigation to installed, automatic valve and timer systems. Your location, landscape theme, style of gardening and budget affect how much water you use and what type of system you should install. Landscapes in hot, dry climates usually require the most extensive irrigation. A sunny lot with an open, southern exposure will generally need more water than a north-facing property with lots of foliage blocking the sun.

Water usage typically rises sharply in the summer, and water prices in dry areas are sometimes increased to discourage excess consumption. Plan your irrigation system to accommodate different levels of seasonal demand and water prices.

The least expensive watering system consists of portable hoses and sprinklers. However, the time and effort spent watering this way are considerable. Automatic timer-controlled watering devices eliminate the chore of dragging hoses and sprinklers around the landscape. Once set up, an automatic system with a timer control will deliver water to all the various elements of the greenscape for the desired length of time and in the correct amount. An automatic timer turns the circuits on and off one at a time, so that the total flow rate doesn't exceed the available gallons per minute from the main water service line. Different emitters deliver water in patterns and volumes suitable for individual plants. Various types of emitters and sprinklers can be combined in a single system, but only if separate circuits are used for each plant group.

Impact Head Used to cover large areas of open lawn and groundcover from corner positions, impact sprayers break up the stream of water and distribute it evenly in an adjustable pattern. These are not appropriate where trees will interrupt even distribution or where the stream of water will injure gardening beds.

Sprinkler Heads Pop-up sprinkler heads deliver water to lawns in quarter-, half- and full-circle patterns. Heads should be adjusted to avoid spraying structures and automobiles and to avoid wasting water on paved surfaces. Low-volume sprinkler heads can be used in garden beds and around shrubs if set to ensure even water distribution.

Drip System The slow, steady flow of water from drip emitters is well suited to trees, shrubs and flower and vegetable beds. Match the drip emitter's flow rate in gallons per hour to the water needs of the individual plant. A drip system is particularly valuable on slopes to avoid excess run-off and in dry climates where water must be conserved.

Bubbler or Shrub Heads Ideal for shrubs, groundcovers and other plants needing regular heavy soakings, bubblers emit a gentle, low-pressure stream of water onto soil beneath individual plants. Bubblers are most effective on level ground.

LAWN SPRINKLERS

Automatic lawn sprinkler systems are methodical to install and use, and they conserve water effectively. The basic parts of the system include the automatic timer, control valves, pipes and pipe fittings, sprinkler heads, risers, anti-siphon valves and drain-out valves for the low end of the circuit if your area freezes in winter.

First test your water pressure at the line between the meter and the house. Then map out your system as a scale drawing, using the base plan. Plot lines and sprinklers along the perimeter of the lawn, using quarter-circle sprinkler heads on the corners, half-circle heads along the edges, and full-circle heads in the middle. Allow some overlap from every head's spray pattern to provide full, even coverage. Make a separate circuit for each section of the yard to be watered separately. After carefully measuring the length of pipe needed and the number of valves and sprinklers required, purchase all of the components.

Your local garden center can be very helpful in planning an in-ground irrigation system. After drawing the layout on your landscape plan, show it to the center's irrigation specialist for help in determining the best heads for your type of plants and garden, and to assure you purchase the proper equipment.

If you have no plumbing experience, tying the sprinkler system into the existing house water lines is probably best left to a professional plumber. If you have some experience, you can install the compression tee, gate valve, anti-siphon valve and manifold (see next page). Once the system is attached to the water lines, you're ready to build the sprinkler system (see pgs. 50–51).

INSTALLING IRRIGATION

Compression Tee and Gate Valve Prior to installation, turn off the water at the meter. Cut the supply line and install a compression tee and a shutoff or gate valve, leaving the supply line to the house undisturbed. Use Teflon tape or pipe compound for water-tight connections.

Anti-Siphon Valve and Manifold Connect an anti-siphon valve to every circuit to prevent backflow of irrigation water into the house drinking water supply. Each valve will control a separate group of sprinklers. All the anti-siphon valves are placed together in a manifold. Each is connected to the main water supply for the system on one side, and to the pipes going out to the circuit on the other.

First Turn off all water, attach pressure gauge to hose bib and open valve to determine the PSI (pressure per sq. in.) and GPM (gal. per min.). PSI should be at least 40. A typical GPM is 12.

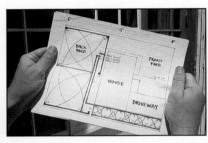

Then Draw irrigation system on the landscape plan. No individual circuit should exceed the total gallons per minute available from the main service.

Third Make complete list of materials. Irrigation system capacity depends on meter size, diameter of service line and water pressure; check specifications with an irrigation specialist before purchase.

Fourth Dig a trench, assembling valves in advance. Install valve systems and check for leaks. Be sure the pipes leading from the anti-siphon valves out to the circuit lines are below ground level.

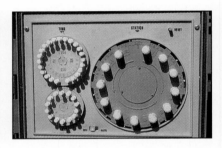

Fifth Install an automatically controlled timer clock, unless manual operation is being used.

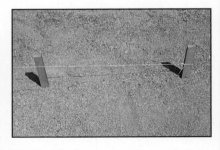

Sixth Mark your system using stakes and string to indicate where to dig lines and install sprinkler heads, leaving 2–3 in. of space near any pavement or walks.

Seventh Dig V-shaped trenches approximately 8 in. deep, or deeper if you have larger pop-up sprinklers. Use a flat-edged spade or trenching machine.

Eighth Assemble each circuit by cutting PVC pipe to length with hacksaw or PVC cutter. Dry fit the pipes first, then join with primer and solvent. Apply to both the inside of the connectors and to the outside of the pipe. Push the pipe in to seat it, rotate 1/4 turn and let it set.

Ninth Lay pipes in trenches. Install risers if required for system. Open the valves to flush out any dirt or debris.

Tenth Adjust pop-up heads to required level. Tops of heads should be at or just below ground level when not in use. Be sure they are completely vertical to allow for uniform spray.

Either Connect impact spray heads for watering of lawn and groundcover areas.

Or Connect drip emitters for trees, shrubs and vegetables needing slow, steady watering.

Or Connect a perforated soaker line for underground watering of hedges and borders.

Next Turn on system and check water coverage or drip rate and adjust as needed.

Last Backfill trench with soil using a spade and smooth surface using a rake.

CAUTION

In freeze areas, use copper pipe from water meter to valves. Always check codes for local restrictions on use of PVC pipe.

SHADE STRUCTURES

Overhead structures provide cool summertime shade for sitting in and enjoying the landscape. Shade structures also provide support for vines and hanging plants and roofing for an outdoor passage from the house to a detached garage or other outbuilding. These structures create enclosed rooms in an outdoor setting.

Arbors, overhead trellises, gazebos and pavilions are among the most popular types of structures for cutting down direct sunlight. Arbors usually extend off the house. Trellises are free standing overhead structures that often have latticework sides attached to post and beam framework. Gazebos are basically rooms without walls often including a foundation and electric power. Pavilions are light outdoor structures, larger than gazebos, suitable for entertaining or enclosing a spa.

Design shade structures to connect the house style to the landscape theme. Build shade structures over bare ground, patios or decks; lawns and sun-loving groundcovers will not survive under the structure. Construction methods vary according to the size and weight of the structure. Traditionally, shade structures have been built of wood. However, structures made of metal posts with canvas roofing can be stunning when they fit the landscape theme. Both wood and metal prefabricated kits are available, often coordinated to spa kits.

SHADE TREES

Large shrubs, tall evergreens and broadleaf shade trees also provide relief from glaring summer sun, but they need time to grow to a size where they can create shade.

A broadleaf, deciduous tree is the best shade choice, with such favorites as maples, beeches and oaks offering the fullest coverage under their protective foliage. In summer the mature tree creates a cool, inviting space beneath its canopy of leaves. In the fall, when the tree begins to lose its leaves, sunlight will find its way through the branches and remaining leaves, and by wintertime, the tree presents only a bare outline of its summertime canopy.

When planting shade trees, consider where their effects are most likely to be needed—adjoining play areas, near the patio or standing alone in the middle of the yard. A shade tree next to the house will cool it off in summer then shed its leaves to let the sun warm it up in winter.

Locate deciduous trees away from pools and ponds to avoid unnecessary leaf cleaning work. Shade trees can create problems for lawn grass and other sun-loving plants growing in their shadows. A lone southern magnolia or other densely leaved shade tree may fit well into an open front yard but kill the grass underneath it. Place deciduous trees where their leaves can be swept up easily, and prune them to provide some sun if you want plants to grow underneath.

LIGHTING DESIGN

Designing the layout of your landscape's illumination requires some knowledge of basic lighting theory. The dramatic mood and emphasis created by your garden lighting will depend on the placement, direction and intensity of the lamps used.

The most aesthetically pleasing effects are usually achieved by low-level illumination with fixtures aimed down and away for soft, indirect light. Backlighting, uplighting and silhouetting should be used more sparingly, since the contrasts and shadows they create tend to exaggerate the shapes of the plants and structures illuminated.

Task lighting is directed at particular areas or structures in order to provide illumination and security for outdoor activities—steps and walkways, driveways, barbecues and patios. Even in these applications, medium-or low-level lighting is preferable to harsh, glaring floodlamps aimed at the eyes.

You should draw a plan for all but the most basic lighting systems. Avoid overloading the fusebox. Always take into account the power consumption of the whole system and the fusebox or circuit breaker to which it is wired. Even with 12 volt systems, the exterior outlets must have GFCI (ground fault circuit interruption) protection. Larger, 120 volt circuits may require a permit and inspection.

Path lighting is most effective when low-voltage lamps are placed at ground level along the perimeter of the walkway.

54

Downlighting can provide security in open areas or contrasting foreground illumination for distant lighted objects.

Uplighting with ground floodlights or well lights will highlight distinctive or unusually shaped trees dramatically.

CAUTION

Mount transformer at least 1' above ground and allow "drip loop" for 120 volt cable to transformer box. All exterior outlet boxes should be waterproofed and GFCI-protected.

Installing a Low-Voltage Light System

First Starting at transformer, set out cable in 50 ft. lengths and place fixtures at desired locations. Leave extra cable for adjustment. Dig trench 4–6 in. deep along path and lay in cable. Consult installation instructions for junction of longer cable.

Next Connect fixtures to cable and test before positioning fixtures permanently.

Last Insert light fixtures and bury cable in soil.

DEFINING EDGES

DIVIDING LINES

To create clean divisions between various elements in the landscape, install edgings where you've drawn the border lines between the areas on the final landscape plan. As a design element, permanent edgings define the forms within the space, accentuate the size of each area and give emphasis to the lines of your landscape. On the practical side, edgings reduce yard work by barring the spread of weeds between planting beds and keep the landscape looking neat and clean by preventing loose fill and soil from spilling between areas.

Select edging materials according to the particular needs of the area. Garden beds can be edged with wood or metal bender board, upright bricks, decorative stones or commercial edging strips. Commercially available edgings are six to ten inch deep strips of steel, polyethylene or heavy-duty aluminum. All of these products will last for years with little or no maintenance. Edgings made of thin corrugated aluminum, bricks laid end up or scalloped cinder blocks are attractive but are not as easy to maintain and may be difficult to mow around.

Mowing strips between lawns and other areas are constructed of brick, flat stone or poured concrete. The edging material is laid level with the edge of the grass so that mower wheels can pass over the surface and leave a precise, neatly trimmed border.

Bricks placed on end create an attractive patterned border to flower beds, paths and other garden areas.

Installing Strip Edgings

First Purchase steel, aluminum, polyethylene or wood strip edging. Dig a trench as deep as the width of the edging between lawn and planting area.

Then Place the edging just above the root zone of the grass, level with the top of the soil.

Next Stake edging in place, securing it at both ends.

Last Backfill and level, leaving soil a maximum 1 in. lower on the planting side.

Pouring a Mowing Strip

First Dig 4 in. deep, 4 in. wide trench with square edges the length of desired mowing strip. Tamp down and level surface.

Then Place form boards along both sides of leveled strip and secure with wood stakes.

Third Mix concrete in wheelbarrow or cement mixer. Pour ready concrete into form.

Fourth Place expansion joint material wherever concrete joins other masonry. Cut 1/4 in. contraction joint every 10 ft. of strip.

Next Use a flat board to level and smooth concrete. Finish surface with flat wood trowel after surface water is gone.

Last Cover with plastic and allow concrete to cure before removing forms.

PREPARING TO PLANT

TESTING THE SOIL

The soil found on new home construction sites is rarely ready for planting. Proper soil drainage is important (see pgs. 32–33), as is soil fertility. If these are not improved, landscape plants will not take root and thrive.

A standard soil fertility test reveals the percentages of nutrients that the soil sample contains, measured as levels of nitrogen (N), phosphorus (P), potassium (K), and level of acidity to alkalinity (pH). These first three are the same numbers that are found in the percent of active ingredients listed on fertilizer labels (for example, 5–10–10). The pH number will tell you how much lime (to correct acidity) or sulfur (to correct alkalinity) are needed.

Community agricultural extension agencies, often associated with state and provincial universities, perform soil tests on samples you provide. Check your telephone directory for the Agricultural Extension Service in your area.

Any imbalance indicated by the soil test requires improvement. Other tests for percolation rate, soil temperature, moisture content and particle size are available, but the NPK and pH levels tell which fertilizers and amendments need to be applied.

Nitrogen promotes good foliage growth and production of chlorophyll. Phosphorus stimulates root system development and enhances flower and seed formation. Potassium helps transport sugars and starches through the plant, building sturdy stems and branches and improving resistance to pests and diseases.

Testing and Amending Soil

First Use hollow soil sampler to extract deep sample of soil; send to Agricultural Extension Service or nursery for testing.

Then Spread recommended amendments over the soil and level surface with a rake.

IMPROVING THE SOIL

To correct any deficiencies revealed by the soil test, add soil amendments. Soil amendments are bulk materials that improve the structure of the soil to allow better drainage, moisture retention and uptake of soil nutrients. Organic materials such as peat moss, humus or compost will correct native soils that are too heavy (mostly clay) or too light (mostly sand). Mix organic amendments into the existing soil at a ratio of between two to one and one to one, depending on the results of drainage and fertility tests. Most amendments except manure are lighter than topsoil, so they create additional pore space and retain water better than heavier materials.

Fertilizers come in several forms: dry granular mixes, liquid mixes and organic materials such as manure, wood ashes, bone meal, cottonseed meal and fish emulsion. For the large soil surfaces of new home landscapes, ready-mixed commercial fertilizers are most practical. Balanced synthetic fertilizers and blended organic fertilizers can be applied with a drop spreader or a hose end sprayer. Bulk organic materials generally have to be spread by hand.

Most landscape plants, grasses, flowers and vegetables prefer a soil pH in the middle of the range, somewhere between 6.5 and 7.5 (7.0 is neutral). Some plants, like ferns and azaleas, thrive in slightly acid soils; a few vegetables grow well in alkaline soils, but a balanced soil is usually best.

Next Turn over soil with shovel, mixing amendments into the soil. For larger areas, use a rotary tiller.

Last Apply fertilizer, and lime or sulfur if needed, with a drop spreader; work into the soil with a shovel or rotary tiller.

SELECTING HEALTHY PLANTS

Inspect landscape plants carefully before purchasing them from a garden center, nursery or landscape contractor. Do not assume that the largest specimen is the best. Younger, smaller plants may, in fact, adapt faster than larger plants. Wait to buy plants until you're ready to install them.

Trunk Injury Avoid trees with a severe injury to the trunk or root system as injuries provide an entrance for disease; the plant may die prematurely. Also, check to see if the top, or leader, has been cut and look for scars or pruning damage.

Healthy Tree A good specimen has a sturdy trunk, well-formed stems, balanced branches and ample foliage, with no signs of disease or pest infestation. Branches should be evenly distributed on all sides.

Poor Shape Misshapen trees should be rejected in favor of better specimens. Look for well-spaced, balanced branches; consult a tree guide for the ideal form of a given species.

Rootbound If the plant has outgrown its container, the roots will be compacted and the tree dwarfed. Avoid split containers and trees with encircling roots at the soil surface or obviously stunted root development.

Healthy Shrub A vigorous specimen should have healthy stems and branches and abundant foliage with good color. Choose shrubs that are well suited to your climate and site conditions.

Healthy Groundcover Nursery flats of spreading groundcover should have well-developed roots, thick plants and profuse foliage. The root system should be fully formed.

Healthy Vine Vines are usually sold when foliage is dense and buds have formed or flowers are blooming; a healthy vine will be well trained around the pole or trellis support.

Poor Shape Shrubs with stunted or broken branches and stems will require creative pruning to grow into handsome landscape plants. To avoid this problem, make sure the shrub conforms to the size and shape of the ideal type before purchase.

Overgrown Groundcover that has been left too long in the flat will have depleted, dry and hardened container soil and may already show dead patches amid the living plants.

Unhealthy Vine If the vine foliage is stunted or yellowed, the leaves show pest damage or blossoms or fruit are dropping too easily, the vine is probably suffering from stress or disease and should be rejected.

Poor Health Pass over shrubs with obvious signs of stress or disease. Yellowing, leaf loss and wilting are a few signs of a plant in poor health.

Too Sparse Groundcover that is immature or too sparse will not transplant well. Watch out for underdeveloped roots that pull out of the soil easily.

Poor Shape Check form and training of the vine structure and the strength of the stems and lower branches at ground level; reject vines that are spindly, broken at the base or top-heavy.

INSTALLING TREES AND SHRUBS

PLANNING FOR GROWTH

Most trees and shrubs grow slowly compared to grasses, groundcovers and vines, but all landscape plants need to be spaced for their final dimensions. Buying small plants and practicing some patience waiting for plants to mature will save you money, since larger specimens are more expensive—and more difficult to install—than smaller ones.

Check with a nursery salesperson or consult a shrub or tree guide for the probable final dimension of each individual specimen. New trees and shrubs need to be spaced far enough apart so that the mature plant will have room to fill out completely without crowding neighboring plants and nearby structures.

Small shrubs can be planted close together, then thinned out after three or four years, if needed. Large shrubs should be spaced with their mature size in mind. Be sure to leave room to move around and between plants for pruning, soil care, treatment of pests and diseases and other maintenance chores.

Nursery-grown trees and shrubs are available either in containers, with burlapped rootballs, or as bare-root specimens in the dormant season; a bare root tree three or four feet tall will weigh a tiny fraction of its counterpart with a full rootball and is far easier to transport than a tree in full bloom. Have help when planting trees and shrubs with heavy rootballs and extensive foliage.

Bare-Root Plantings

First Prune damaged or diseased roots. Dig a hole 6 in. wider than the root system and 1 in. shallower than the plant's length from the bottom of the roots and the soil line on the trunk.

Next Mix necessary amendments with soil from the hole. Set plant in hole. Soil line on the trunk should be 1 in. higher than ground level.

Last Press soil over roots. Fill hole halfway with soil. Water to settle soil. Finish filling hole with soil. Mound soil basin around plant.

Container Plantings

First Moisten soil and allow to drain. Bang on container to loosen rootball. Remove nursery stakes. Supporting trunk, slide container from rootball.

Next Trim any circling roots. Dig hole as deep as the root ball and twice as wide. Mix amendments with soil from hole.

Last Set plant in hole with soil line on trunk at ground level. Place a stake on either side of trunk; secure trunk to stakes with gardener's tape. Fill in hole with amended soil, build water basin at diameter of rootball and water well. Remove supports after first year.

Balled and Burlapped Plantings

First Dig hole as deep as the rootball and twice as wide. Mix amendments with soil from hole.

Next Holding rootball firmly, lower plant into hole. Cut, but do not remove bag, and trim any circling roots. Caution: large rootballs are very heavy.

Last Position plant so that soil line on trunk is at ground level. Place a stake on either side of trunk; secure trunk to stakes with gardener's tape. Fill hole with amended soil, build water basin at diameter of rootball and water well. Remove supports after first year.

INSTALLING VINES AND CLIMBERS

VERTICAL SPACE

Vines, climbing roses and other upward-growing plants utilize the landscape's vertical space. Climbing plants can be grown along fences and trellises, trained on frames in formal or informal patterns, or allowed to wander freely over shade structures. Vines and climbers soften the appearance of built surfaces; chain link fences, propane tanks, large expanses of house walls and other unsightly objects in the landscape can be disguised by their foliage.

There are several methods by which vines and other climbers grow, which determine the type of structure they can be grown on. Some vines produce aerial rootlets like suction cups, which attach themselves to flat surfaces. Other vines produce twining tendrils, which must be trained on slender wires or plastic mesh. Still other types have twining leaf stems that will grow around medium-sized supports. Climbing roses and other rambling, thorny stemmed plants will climb to great heights if you train and tie them with gardener's tape to solid supports.

For a more artful treatment of vertical space, espaliers create a living pattern on walls and fences. Classic espaliers have geometric forms onto which the vines are laboriously trained; informal variations create a more natural effect. Fruit trees, vines and many shrubs can be trained and shaped as espaliers.

Train climbing plants into *espalier* by tying the vines to a wire or wooden frame and trimming the excess foliage to reveal the desired pattern. The result is a striking display set against the backdrop of a wall or fence.

Aerial Rootlets Ivy clings to flat wall surfaces with aerial rootlets. Ivy looks good on any brick or stucco home and fits particularly well with Traditional American landscape themes. Beware of ivy roots wearing away wood and masonry.

Twining Stems Fast-growing clematis stems twine themselves around medium-strength trellis and wire supports. Big blossoms on vines growing over 10 ft. tall are a colorful adornment for bare exterior walls.

Twining Tendrils Support the delicate twining tendrils and multicolored flowers of sweet pea with thin wire or plastic mesh screen. Vines serve as an effective backdrop to flower gardens.

Climbing Roses Vertically growing roses like Climbing Joseph's Coat and Climbing White Dawn need to be trained and tied to supports. Use climbing and rambler roses as brilliant color accents for the summer garden.

INSTALLING GROUNDCOVERS

LAWN ALTERNATIVES

Where grass lawns are not appropriate, an expanse of groundcover plants offers an interesting alternative. Groundcovers are low-growing perennial plants that spread across horizontal surfaces, knitting together into a solid carpet of vegetation. They provide erosion control, colorful seasonal flowers and sweet fragrances over irregular surfaces. Groundcovers are available in a wide range of leaf and flower types, and once they are well established require little maintenance.

Groundcovers work particularly well on rocky surfaces and on areas designated for low-maintenance. They can be started in the gaps of outdoor walls; groundcovers will eventually wind their way around rocks and into nooks and crannies, trailing down vertical surfaces and spreading out over horizontal ones. Groundcovers adapt to any landscape theme.

Groundcovers are usually purchased in nursery flats, in which groups of plants are clumped together, but they are also available as seeds and as sod or plugs in some cases. The plants in flats have to be separated and planted individually in order to cover a large surface area economically. Each plant will send out runners that intertwine and eventually form a solid cover of green.

Planting Groundcover from Flats

First Turn necessary amendments into soil with spading shovel.

Then Rake soil clean of rocks and debris and level.

Third Using a dull knife, towel or spade, separate clumps of groundcover gently.

Fourth Set plants out in checkerboard pattern for maximum coverage.

Next Dig hole 4 in. or larger for each plug. Place plugs in holes and firm soil.

Last Water plants well with overhead sprayer to settle soil.

Used in low traffic areas where lawn grass is not practical, groundcovers solve a number of design problems. They don't need continuous maintenance, offer an alternative to the texture and color of grass and can trail down and around ledges, walls and rocky nooks.

INSTALLING TURF AND LAWN

GREEN GRASS AT HOME

A handsome lawn is a traditional element of many home landscapes, serving to unify the greenscape and creating a comfortable open space suitable for a wide range of outdoor activities. While the chores and expense involved in maintaining a large lawn can be intimidating, proper planning will help.

The cost of a lawn includes initial installation costs—soil amendments, grass and irrigation—and the cost of watering and fertilizing over the lawn's lifetime.

Maintenance time is dependent on how you plan to water the lawn as well as the frequency of mowing, fertilizing and trimming. Installed irrigation systems with timer controls lessen watering time considerably. Mow strips lessen mowing and trimming times, too. All costs are dependent on the size of the lawn.

Before planting a new lawn, select a type of grass suited to your climate. Grass is broadly classified as either "cool season" or "warm season." Discuss the best type to meet your needs with your local supplier.

There are four ways to install grass—as seed, sod, sprigs or plugs. Sowing seed is the least expensive and gives the greatest variety, although it takes months to produce a lawn. Sodding is the quickest way to get a solid carpet of grass, and the most expensive. Plugs or sprigs of grass are less costly than sod, but they also take months to get established.

To calculate the cost of installation, measure the lawn area in square feet, adding about ten percent extra for sod, sprigs and plugs. Be prepared to water every day for the first few weeks after planting while the lawn gets established.

Seeding

First After preparing and leveling the soil, sow grass seeds evenly across soil surface using drop spreader. Cover area twice at 90° angles.

Next Gently rake surface using back of landscape rake. Use a roller over the surface.

Last Lightly mulch by hand. Water with fine spray 1–3 times a day until established. Barricade lawn from passersby.

Sodding

First Before purchasing, inspect to ensure that sod is moist, not sopping wet or dry and cracked. Prepare and level the soil before planting.

Next Fit strips tightly to surface. Do not overlap, but avoid gaps. Cut to fit around any obstacles using a sharp knife.

Last Press sod into soil bed with half-filled lawn roller in 3 passes. Keep constantly moist until established. Barricade lawn from passersby.

PLANTING SEASONAL LANDSCAPES

FLOWER GARDENING

Colorful flowering plants are available as annuals, perennials, bulbs and flowering shrubs, vines and groundcovers. Flowers can be used for seasonal displays such as rose or rhododendron gardens, in cutting gardens used for flower arrangements, to define edges and enclose spaces and as decorative landscape accents in beds, borders or containers. Seasonal sequences need to be planned to produce year-round color.

Annuals are single-season plants that are usually grown from seed and planted in spring. Hardy annuals like larkspur are sometimes planted in fall for spring flowers. Forget-me-nots and petunias can be pinched back to bloom through summer and fall.

Perennials are longer lasting plants that live through the winter to bloom again, year after year. Clumping perennials such as lupine and dianthus create colorful backdrops for bulbs and annuals, making it possible for the clever gardener to have constantly changing color throughout the growing season.

Some spring flowering bulbs—tulips, daffodils, lilies—are also hardy perennials and will bloom year after year. In some climates summer flowering bulbs such as gladiolus, dahlias, and tuberous begonias need to be dug up after they bloom and kept in a cool, dry place for replanting in the spring. The composition of your garden will be dependent on the climate in your area.

Planting Flowering Bulbs

First Dig hole between 4 and 24 in. deep, depending on bulb type. Amend soil as needed.

Then Place bulb in hole with points up. Cover with soil and water well. After blooming, allow plant to completely die back before trimming off foliage.

Planting Annual Transplants

First When plants have 3–4 sets of leaves, harden outdoors in a coldframe or on a screen porch by exposing gradually to outdoor conditions.

Then Use a trowel to make hole deep and wide enough to place plant. Amend soil as needed.

Third Water plants in container to retain soil for easier removal. Remove plant from container by pressing on the sides and the bottom. Ease plant out.

Fourth Retain as much soil as possible around the roots. Set plant into hole with soil line at ground level.

Next Press soil firmly around plant and water gently but thoroughly.

Last If sun is intense, protect transplant with shade protection. Water daily until plant is established.

CARING FOR THE NEW LANDSCAPE

GENERAL MAINTENANCE

Every element of the new landscape has different care and maintenance needs. The time spent on upkeep pays for itself by protecting your investment.

The elements of the hardscape need regular inspection to see that erosion, rust and breakage are not affecting the equipment or material. Confirm that automatic and timer-controlled systems are operating correctly. Check light fixtures for breakage, chewed wires and short circuits. Inspect the irrigation system periodically.

Check wood surfaces for infestation by termites and other pests, and protect them with an all-weather sealer if necessary. Inspect concrete surfaces for cracking and movement, even if new. Protect metal surfaces on lawn furniture, sheds and light fixtures from rust with paint or sealant.

Maintain the soil to ensure that plants are vigorous (see pgs. 74–75). Keep debris and leaves cleaned up to prevent pests and diseases from gaining a foothold. Amend soil with decomposed compost and other fertilizers seasonally. Lawn soil may need periodic restoration, such as aeration, liming and renewal with soil amendments.

The best way to organize your program is with a well-planned maintenance schedule. Every chore can be noted down on a garden calendar to remind you when it's time to perform weekly, monthly, seasonal and annual landscape maintenance tasks.

The new greenscape needs a year-round program of watering, fertilizing and disease and pest control. The hardscape needs maintenance, too. Utility and irrigation lines are vulnerable to freezing and cracking. Wood, concrete and metal surfaces benefit from protection from the effects of extreme weather.

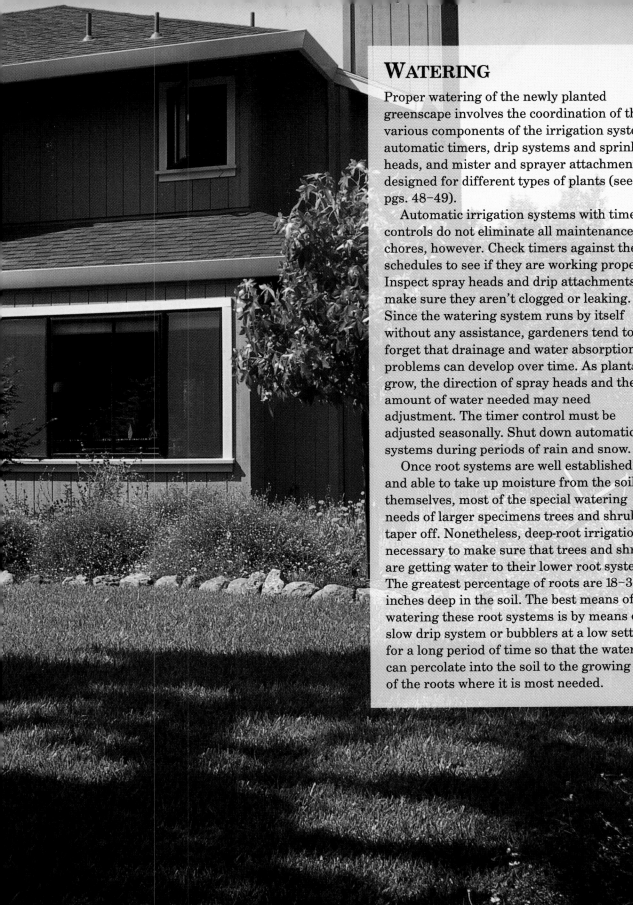

WATERING

Proper watering of the newly planted greenscape involves the coordination of the various components of the irrigation system: automatic timers, drip systems and sprinkler heads, and mister and sprayer attachments designed for different types of plants (see pgs. 48–49).

Automatic irrigation systems with timer controls do not eliminate all maintenance chores, however. Check timers against their schedules to see if they are working properly. Inspect spray heads and drip attachments to make sure they aren't clogged or leaking. Since the watering system runs by itself without any assistance, gardeners tend to forget that drainage and water absorption problems can develop over time. As plants grow, the direction of spray heads and the amount of water needed may need adjustment. The timer control must be adjusted seasonally. Shut down automatic systems during periods of rain and snow.

Once root systems are well established and able to take up moisture from the soil by themselves, most of the special watering needs of larger specimens trees and shrubs taper off. Nonetheless, deep-root irrigation is necessary to make sure that trees and shrubs are getting water to their lower root systems. The greatest percentage of roots are 18–36 inches deep in the soil. The best means of watering these root systems is by means of a slow drip system or bubblers at a low setting for a long period of time so that the water can percolate into the soil to the growing tips of the roots where it is most needed.

73

MAINTAINING PLANTS

CARING FOR TREES

Newly planted trees need protection, nurturing and pruning in order to grow into mature, vigorous specimens. Because trees are the backbone of the greenscape—and likely the most expensive elements of your landscape—proper soil, water and light conditions must be considered carefully when planning the location of each tree.

Protect young trees from birds, deer and other animals; new plantings are more vulnerable to predators and pests than well-established ones. To protect a fragile young tree against wind damage, install a stake on either side of the trunk and tie the trunk to the stakes with gardener's tape, or use guy wires attached to a removable rubber hose collar around the trunk. Remove supports after the first year.

Pruning and training give trees good shape and healthy foliage. Prune young trees selectively, to remove dead or broken branches or correct obvious structural weaknesses. Select sturdy, well-placed vertical limbs for permanent branches, and leave some lower branches and foliage to protect the immature trunk from sunscald.

Trees are considered mature after four or five years. The mature tree requires a different approach to pruning. Annually cut off all dead or disease-weakened limbs; thin out excess foliage and crossed or broken branches. If the young tree is pruned and shaped correctly, less pruning will be needed on the mature tree.

Eventually trees may grow beyond the scale of the yard. Although removing a healthy tree is a difficult decision to make, keep the principles of design (see pgs. 6–7) in mind as the landscape grows, just as in planning the landscape initially.

CARING FOR SHRUBS

Shrubs require well-timed pruning and fertilizing for vigor. Never let the outer dimensions of a shrub grow much beyond the final size and shaped desired. Hedges should be pruned regularly from planting to establish a thick habit of growth.

Prune evergreen shrubs by shortening new growth. If you cut beyond the new growth, the foliage will not grow back. Prune spring-flowering shrubs only after they finish blooming. Prune summer- and fall-blooming shrubs in the late winter or early spring. Begin by removing any dead, broken or disease-weakened branches. Then thin out excess branches and foliage to restore the shrub to its desired form, opening up the inner branches and foliage to the sun. Clip off protruding stems and crossed branches and pinch back the shoots to promote foliage growth and new blossoms. Wait until the dormant season to prune again.

Once the growing season has begun, give the shrub a boost by applying a balanced dry fertilizer to the surrounding soil, or applying liquid fertilizer in solution around the drip line. Perform direct foliar feeding in the morning or on overcast days; don't leave the shrub wet overnight, especially in moist, humid climates.

Spring is the best time to add soil amendments. Add a mulch around the base of the shrub to assist in water retention in the summer during dry, hot spells. This is also a good time for deep-root irrigation.

CARING FOR LAWNS

Lawns need regular mowing, fertilizing, weeding and pest control to stay healthy. Begin your maintenance program as soon as the lawn is established.

Mow lawns when the blades reach about one-third higher than the desired height. Don't mow when grass is wet and slippery; the clippings will be heavy, and the grass will get matted down by the mower.

Fertilize lawns in spring and fall. The easiest way to apply dry lawn fertilizer is with a drop spreader; apply liquid lawn fertilizers from a hose-end sprayer or through the irrigation system. Follow label directions to avoid burning the lawn with chemicals.

Destroy weeds with pre-emergent herbicides that kill sprouting weeds as they reach the soil surface, or post-emergent herbicides that kill broadleaf weeds selectively. Isolated patches of weeds are more safely and easily removed by hand weeding. Warm season grasses should be dethatched every few years to remove dead roots, stems and other debris. If thatch gets too heavy, use a lawn aerator to loosen the soil surface for better irrigation and air circulation.

The best defense against lawn pests and diseases is always preventive maintenance, through proper mowing, watering and feeding procedures. Try dethatching and mowing the lawn, removing all clippings, watering heavily and applying nitrogen before resorting to chemical controls. Inspect closely to identify which pest you are dealing with; if the cleanup fails to eliminate the pest or disease, apply insecticides or other treatments, following the manufacturer's directions carefully.

CARING FOR FLOWER BEDS

Flowering plants are in a constant process of change and renewal. Where annuals, perennials and bulbs are mixed in a single garden bed, maintenance can be tricky unless you know where everything is. Mark the sites of the various flower groups with tags and make a map of the flower beds showing precise locations.

In spring, gently cultivate the garden soil, working with hand tools to avoid damaging shallow roots. Wait until bulbs are up before cultivating areas where they are planted. Turn over the bare soil and mix in a balanced 10-10-10 fertilizer to stimulate growth. Later in the year use a fertilizer low in nitrogen.

Meanwhile, turn your attention to pest and disease control. Aphids, fungal diseases and wilts are particularly difficult to control in humid climates. Hand-picking bugs and spraying aphids and mites with water can be effective, but serious infestations may require chemical pesticides. When snails and slugs are too numerous to remove by hand, use chemical pellets or powders.

Gophers, deer and other animal pests can wreak havoc by digging up bulbs and eating flowers and leaves. Screen, net and fence barriers will keep out unwelcome small intruders.

To keep flower beds looking fresh, delay seed production and prolong flowering, practice deadheading throughout the blooming season. To deadhead, just snip or pinch off the faded flowers and discard them.

In fall, clear flower beds of all leaves, dead plants and other debris so that pests don't have a place to hibernate. If weather permits, grow winter-blooming perennials for year-round color.

ENJOYING YOUR HOME

After the landscape has evolved into its mature form, you will be able to appreciate all the effort that went into its design and installation, and so will everyone else who sees it. With proper care, your enjoyment should last for many years to come.

LANDSCAPE PROFESSIONALS

Landscaping succeeds if all the steps of design and installation are followed carefully. If you aren't sure how to deal with a particular problem, there are professionals available to help. You will get the most from the money you pay professionals if you are clear about what you want from your landscape before meeting with them.

Landscape architects are qualified professionals who design and direct the installation of hardscapes and greenscapes. They usually specialize in either commercial or residential projects or in specific styles of landscaping. Check to see if they are members of the American Society of Landscape Architects.

Landscape designers—often horticulture experts—usually specialize in designing residential landscaping but do not participate in its installation. Landscape contractors are licensed to install hardscapes and greenscapes; they may be able to help with the design. Gardeners and landscape maintenance services perform more routine gardening and cleanup chores.

All professionals should provide contracts specifying fees and expenses, materials costs and dates of completion. Take bids on larger jobs involving subcontracting or when special services are required.

In addition to these landscape professionals, there are a host of other qualified experts who can assist you in the long-term care of the landscape. County extension agents, nursery professionals and local gardening clubs are an invaluable source of advice and information. Specialists in irrigation, pond and pool construction and tree pruning and removal can assist with these large projects.

INDEX

A Note From NK Lawn and Garden Co.

For more than 100 years, since its founding in Minneapolis, Minnesota, NK Lawn and Garden has provided gardeners with the finest quality seed and other garden products.

We doubt that our leaders, Jesse E. Northrup and Preston King, would recognize their seed company today, but gardeners everywhere in the U.S. still rely on NK Lawn and Garden's knowledge and experience at planting time.

We are pleased to be able to share this practical experience with you through this ongoing series of easy-to-use gardening books.

Here you'll find hundreds of years of gardening experience distilled into easy-to-understand text and step-by-step pictures. Every popular gardening subject is included.

As you use the information in these books, we hope you'll also try our lawn and garden products. They're available at your local garden retailer.

There's nothing more satisfying than a successful, beautiful garden. There's something special about the color of blooming flowers and the flavor of home-grown garden vegetables.

We understand how special you feel about growing things—and NK Lawn and Garden feels the same way, too. After all, we've been a friend to gardeners everywhere since 1884.